About the Author.

Hester Bancroft is a well-known coach, therapist and motivational speaker who is passionate about assisting individuals wishing to establish more positive ways of living their lives. Hester facilitates transformational changes within her clients through dealing with the underlying causes of existing unhelpful behaviours, establishing empowering new behaviours and setting attainable and sustainable goals for the future.

Hester has a first class degree in Psychology, is a Master Practitioner of Neuro-linguistic Programming (NLP) and is a member of the British Psychological Society. She is also currently undertaking doctoral studies with the world-renowned Metanoia Institute in London.

Hester Bancroft
BSc (hons) Psych, M Prac NLP, MBPsS

Dedication

To all the wonderful women who nurture and support the people around them; this book is a reminder to also nurture and support yourself. Honour your needs, embrace your passions and cherish your dreams.

Hester Bancroft

LIFE COACHING IN YOUR POCKET
(FOR WOMEN)
TAKE STOCK OF THE SIX KEY AREAS OF YOUR LIFE

AUSTIN MACAULEY
PUBLISHERS LTD.

A CIP catalogue record for this title is available from the British Library.

ISBN 978 1 78455 130 8

www.austinmacauley.com

First Published (2015)
Austin Macauley Publishers Ltd.
25 Canada Square
Canary Wharf
London
E14 5LB

Printed and bound in Great Britain

Acknowledgments

Thank-you to my husband, Simon, for his unwavering love, support and encouragement and for making me smile each and every day. Also thank-you to my three beautiful children, Zoe, Jessica and Max who have each, in their own unique and wonderful way, brought such joy, purpose and happiness into my life. Finally, thank-you to my dear friend Claire whose wisdom and humour has meant so much to me for so many years.

CONTENTS

INTRODUCTION

As women our lives are forever changing; after school or university we will probably work, we might then commit to a long-term partner, marry, have children, stop work altogether for a while or work part-time. As our children grow, we might then return full-time to the workplace or (as is increasingly common) retrain and begin a second career.

Whilst managing and navigating these distinctly different phases in our lives, our focus tends to be almost exclusively on supporting those in our care: whether that is our partner, our children or, as we get older, our own parents. This focus on other people's needs can make it scarily easy for us, as women, to lose sight of what we ourselves want and need from life.

To create the life we desire we must have a really good understanding of not only what is going on for us right now, but also what we would *like* to be going on for us, in all areas of our lives, in the future. Allowing ourselves time to stand back and focus on what it is we need is crucial if we wish to move forward feeling content and truly happy.

There are six key areas in life that we all need to regularly invest in. Each chapter in this book covers a key area and will give you the opportunity to explore each area in depth.

At the end of each chapter you will also have the opportunity to set some attainable and sustainable goals for the future.

Self-awareness

A major focus of this book is on increasing self-awareness. Self-awareness allows us to not only understand ourselves at a deeper level, but also to recognise and utilise our unique skills and abilities to the very best of our ability.

Throughout this book then, I will be posing questions to you that will allow you to gain a deeper understanding of yourself, your relationships and how you are organising and spending your time. I will also be sharing some key communication and listening skills; skills that, when used, will enhance each and every one of your relationships.

Self-reflection

As we all know, self-reflection is a necessary part of any change, so in order to get the most out of this book, I urge you to allow yourself the time you need to reflect on your answers; really open your heart and mind to new possibilities and new ways of 'being' in light of what you learn about yourself. It would also be useful to keep a notebook and pen with this book in order that you can record your answers to the exercises as you do them. Having a notepad handy will also allow you to note down any additional thoughts and realisations you have along the way.

Your comfort zone and beyond

When we are looking to make changes, it is also crucially important to consider our current willingness to step outside our comfort zone. In our comfort zone we feel relaxed, capable and competent and it is necessary for all of us to have these times when we feel totally at ease. However, if we wish to develop ourselves and to grow as people, it is also important for us to also be willing to regularly step outside our comfort zones. In addition, staying *only* within our comfort zone can ultimately leave us feeling bored, unchallenged and unfulfilled.

When we step outside our comfort zone we enter what is known as our 'stretch' zone (or some people call it our 'learning' zone). Here we put ourselves in situations that feel uncomfortable *but manageable*. In this zone we tend to feel both excited and nervous; when we have achieved our 'mission' we often feel exhilarated and (quite rightly) pleased with ourselves; we may even wish to do it all over again! Importantly, the more we repeat something in our stretch zone the easier it is and the bigger our comfort zone becomes. There is, of course, a risk when we step outside our comfort zone; things *may* not work out as we want them to. If this happens it is crucial we take the learning from the experience and, if our goal is important to us, consider alternative ways to reach it.

Some of our biggest goals in life may be *beyond* our stretch zone in what is known as our 'stress' zone (or some people call it our 'danger' zone). This is the zone where we can feel overwhelmed and anxious and can experience a very strong desire to return (as quickly as possible) to our comfort zone. Our biggest goals, therefore, need to be reached by the continued expansion of our comfort zones. Those tentative but exhilarating steps outside our comfort zone allow us ultimately to access the zone where the magic happens.

It would be useful to spend a moment reflecting on how many times, during the last month, you have stepped outside your own personal comfort zone; consider whether you are currently taking those steps on a regular enough basis or whether it would be beneficial for you to do so even more frequently.

Big picture

Before we delve into our first key area, it would be useful now to focus on some overarching questions about what is going on for you at this point in your life.

Exercise 1/0

• **What do you currently have in your life that you no longer want?**

• **What do you currently *not* have in your life that you *now* want?**

• **When, where and with whom are you at your absolute happiest? (Think here of all of the different situations when you are, of have been, truly happy)**

• **What is your vision of a fulfilling life?**

• **What are the key things you would like to achieve in your lifetime?**

We will now begin our journey.

CHAPTER 1

INTIMATE RELATIONSHIPS

Whether we are currently in an intimate relationship or not, this is the starting point of our exploration. Our intimate relationships, past and present, are an enormously important part of our history; whilst they should not define us, they *do* shape us as they affect our values and beliefs about love, trust and commitment.

All of us carry out our roles in the world differently – how we 'do' relationships – as a partner, mother, daughter, friend or work colleague. Recognising what roles we take on allows us to look back over time and spot our behavioural patterns, the things we do time and time again – whether they are helpful or not.

Think for a moment about the roles we might take on in our intimate relationships; we may tend to take the adult role (or indeed, the child role) instead of holding an expectation that the relationship should be equally and mutually supportive. We may take on the needy role; seeking or asking for constant reassurance or conversely, we may take on the fiercely independent and distant role. Sometimes we assume the role of the rescuer; wanting to shield our partner from life's difficulties, or we may be someone always looking to be rescued.

When we understand the role we take on in our intimate relationships, it helps us to bring a new self-awareness to our other relationships, as we will see echoes of these roles being played out in different ways with different people. Only when we stop to examine how we do relationships can we choose to do them even better, perhaps even entirely differently.

Exercise 1/1

Think now about your relationship or, if you are single, think about your last significant relationship (going back in time to when you were with that person prior to being in the throes of your break-up):

- **What do you love and admire about this person?**
- **What do you really enjoy doing together?**
- **What does your partner do that makes you feel loved?**
- **What would make you feel even more loved?**
- **What do you find tricky about the relationship?**
- **Is there anything that you would like this person to really, really understand about you that they don't currently understand?**

These questions will highlight to you what it is that you appreciate about your partner, as well as the aspects you may find hard. They will also highlight to you your 'love evidence'; the things that make you feel cherished and adored (whether that is a thoughtful gift, physical affection, being told how special you, feeling truly listened to or something entirely different).

Exploring and expressing one another's love evidence is an important part of relationship coaching because, very often, we assume that what makes us feel loved will also make our partner feel loved. The reality is that their love evidence may be something entirely different. It is, therefore, hugely beneficial for both partners to understand what their partner needs in order to feel loved and appreciated.

If we think of every relationship we have as a well choreographed dance it allows us to understand our part in creating each relationship we have. None of us can expect another person to change their way of being (their way of dancing with us) without us changing our side of the dance. Understanding this is hugely empowering; put simply, when we change our behaviour (*our way of dancing*) our partner has to change theirs, in order to keep dancing.

So now I would like you to think about how you would like to 'dance' in your relationship. If you are not in a great place with your partner you may feel that, right now, they don't deserve you being the very best you can be. However, this journey of discovery is not about your partner, it is about you and your personal vision of your best.

Exercise 2/1

When (and if) you were feeling totally and utterly in love and as happy as you could possibly be:

- **What kind of partner would you like to be?**

- **How would you like to make your partner feel?**

- **What would you like to feel you give to them in terms of support?**

- **Do you know a woman who you admire for her way of being in her relationship?**

- **What is it about her way of being that you would like to replicate?**

These things reflect your vision of the dance you want to dance; your beliefs about what one partner should give to the other.

Exercise 3/1

Think now about how your partner might dance with you if you were consistently dancing this dance:

- **Would they be surprised?**

- **How do you think they would respond to you?**

- **What changes do you think might occur within the relationship?**

Another important part of relationship coaching is helping each person in the relationship to explore and communicate his or her personal boundaries. Even if we have never thought about it, all of us have boundaries in every relationship; specific behaviours that are not acceptable to us because we find them hurtful, infuriating or abhorrent. It is incredibly helpful to have clarity around our boundaries so that we become not only excellent at communicating them but also comfortable enforcing them. The ability to do these things directly affects how happy and secure we can feel within our relationship.

Exercise 4/1

Think now about *your* boundaries and make a list of what behaviours are unacceptable to you. It would then be useful to number them in order of importance. Once you have done this, consider how many times a person could break through a boundary and still have forgiveness from you.

Some behaviours may be so unacceptable that once would be the limit, while others may be a 'three strikes and you're out' type behaviour. There are no rights or wrongs here; your boundaries are unique to *you* and your ability to forgive reflects how much importance you personally place on the behaviour.

Exercise 5/1

Now return to thinking about your relationship (or last significant relationship):

• **How good are you at communicating your boundaries?**

• **How good are you at letting your partner know they have gone through a boundary?**

• **Crucially, do you feel your partner regularly goes through your boundaries and that you are powerless to stop them?**

21

As we all know, the calmer we are when communicating *anything* we wish to communicate, the better chance we have of being heard. It is important to be clear and specific about what our boundaries are and to provide an explanation as to why we feel the way we do. Explaining why a boundary is important to us personally and how we would feel if our partner went through that boundary removes any feeling that we are attacking or criticising them and facilitates open and honest discussion.

If a partner has gone through a boundary or, indeed, done anything to hurt, frustrate or anger us, the way we communicate our feelings is crucial to how successfully we manage the situation. If we use 'I' statements (e.g. 'I feel really hurt that...') rather than 'you' statements (e.g. 'You did X and then you did Y...') we will *always* get a better result. When any of us feel we are being accused or blamed for something, we tend to go straight into denial or justification. However, when someone tells us how he or she is *feeling* (even if it is furious) we cannot deny their feelings (they belong to that person *not* to us) and we tend to feel less attacked and much more able to talk about the situation.

If you feel your partner does not respect your boundaries it is important to think about your part (however small) in creating the situation.

Exercise 6/1

• **Do you let things go rather than draw attention to something that is upsetting you?**

- Do you tend to shout or nag rather than explain how you are feeling in a clear and calm manner?

- Do you ever play the role of martyr?

- Are you choosing to remain in a relationship with someone who has no respect for your boundaries, and if so, why?

Next Steps…

Giving thought to all of the above allows you to truly take stock of where you are in your intimate relationship. It would be useful, now, for you to answer these goal-setting questions in light of any new awareness you may have gained from doing the previous exercises.

Exercise 7/1

Goal Setting for your intimate relationship:

- What, if anything, will you change about the role you play in your relationship?

- Do you need to get an increased understanding of what makes your partner feel loved and valued?

- What specifically, if anything, will you change about the dance you dance?

- What, if anything, do you need to do to improve how you communicate your personal boundaries?

Goal setting for those who are currently single but wish to be in a relationship:

If you are currently single but wish to be in a relationship, you are now in a great position to think about your ideal future partner. I urge you to be greedy with this because we really do tend to get what we focus on.

Make a list now of the top ten things that are crucial to you about a partner; what kind of person would you like them to be and what kind of role do you want them to have in your life? Ensure that everything on the list is stated in the positive (e.g. rather than 'I don't want them to be controlling' put 'I want them to be accepting of my life and independence').

Once you have written your list (known as your 'relationship values'), rank them in order of importance; really take your time over this – remember it will help you to draw the kind of person you want into your life.

Finally list the sorts of places where this person might be, where they might spend their time. Then think about whether you are ever in those places or whether you need to add different activities into your life in order to create the opportunities for you to meet your new partner.

An important note...

Finally, it is important for all of us to recognise that it is not our partner's responsibility to make us happy; happiness really does come from inside. Our partner is the companion we have chosen to share our journey with. In a healthy relationship, our partner will enhance our life; they give us love and affection, share new experiences, support us when things are tough, and share our joy when things go well, all of which can add to our happiness enormously.

When (and if) we come out of a significant relationship it is hugely beneficial to spend some time alone before embarking on a new relationship. This gives us time to learn how to be happy and secure in ourselves. It is when we feel strong enough to stand on our own two feet (physically, emotionally and financially) that we are truly able to make empowered decisions about how we wish to live our lives. If we rely on a new partner to make us feel happy or secure we are in real danger of making ill-fated decisions based on need rather than purely considering whether a prospective partner has the ability to add to our happiness and our enjoyment of life.

Whatever our current situation, it is when we take full responsibility for creating our own happiness that we can ensure that our intimate relationship is the best it can be.

As Richard Bach, the American writer, once said:

"Every person, all the events of your life are there because you have drawn them there. What you choose to do with them is up to you."

CHAPTER 2

CAREER AND PERSONAL DEVELOPMENT

This chapter will allow you to explore how your career has developed so far, what is going on for you right now, and how you would like your career to develop in the future. It will also give you the opportunity to focus on your core skills and passions to ensure you are developing yourself in ways that are truly meaningful to you.

We have touched on how, as women, our lives are forever changing; distinct phases of our working lives are created by events such as marriage, pregnancy, logistics of childcare and (increasingly commonly for many of us) divorce and subsequent relationships.

For the majority of women our home and family lives have a crucial bearing on all the choices we make; we often accept lesser-paid or lower-graded positions to fit in with school days and holidays or take complete career breaks in order to care for our children. In addition, if our partner's job changes or relocates, we often move further away from our own contacts and previous working environments. Not surprisingly then, many women consider retraining and go on to embrace second careers due to changes in their circumstances, priorities and (very often) their increased understanding of themselves.

Wherever you are yourself right now (working full or part-time, at home, married or single, parent or not) I am sure that, as a woman, you will have made choices based on the needs of others. So, whilst fully accepting that the logistics of our family lives and the maintenance of our key relationships have an important bearing on our career and personal development choices, I urge you to give yourself permission to focus only on your own needs as you work through the exercises in this chapter and let your own, inner voice, be the loudest.

Let's look at you

Firstly let's revisit our childhood and get back in touch with what hopes and dreams we had for ourselves before adulthood, limiting beliefs or stark reality took over.

Between the approximate ages of seven and fourteen, each and every one of us goes through the 'modelling' phase. This is the phase when we actively seek out role models: people we know, see or read about whom we wish to emulate.

Think back to this time now and focus on the childhood ambitions you had for yourself (however fleeting or seemingly whimsical). Our adult selves can be very quick to dismiss our childhood dreams as ridiculous, sometimes to the extent that we forget we even had them, so when you answer the questions below, really allow yourself time and indulge yourself fully; those ideas were there even if some *now* seem outlandish, unrealistic or even utterly impossible.

The (probably diverse) roles you thought about as a child will have key elements that specifically appealed to you at the time; some roles may have a caring element, some glamorous, some influential, some exciting, some may allow you to perform, some to travel, some to be heroic and some to be part of a team or a respected institute. These were the elements that resonated with you as a child and (*at some level*) will still resonate with you now.

Exercise 1/2

Think now about the following questions:

- **What different jobs, roles, careers you have ever thought about, dreamed about or just imagined doing?**
- **Are there any common elements in those roles?**
- **Do you currently have any of these elements in your life?**
- **If you could choose just one of those elements to add into your life now, what would it be?**

Now, think about people you currently admire for what they do, for how they behave or for the skills they may have. Again, these can be people you know or have just seen or read about (they may not even be alive today). Even as adults, it is useful for us to be aware of who we admire in the world and why.

Exercise 2/2

For those people, think about the following:

- **What specifically are the things you admire about each of them?**
- **What characteristics or skills do they have that you would most like to emulate?**
- **What would you need to do, have or learn to be able to do that?**

As women, and particularly as mothers, we can focus on those we support and, naturally, feel proud of their achievements. In doing so, though, we can sometimes forget to focus on our own achievements, so I would like you now to think about everything you have achieved so far in your life (big or small): from your school life all the way through to now.

Exercise 3/2

- **Which, of all those things, are you proudest of?**
- **What enabled you to achieve it?**
- **How did you *feel* when you achieved it?**

Really take time to acknowledge and enjoy the feeling of having achieved all that you have; these feelings can provide us with fantastic motivation to achieve more.

Before we focus on the specifics of your career and personal development I would like you to ponder some key questions.

Exercise 4/2

• **What has been the happiest period of your working life?**

• **What was it about that period that made it so enjoyable?**

• **If money didn't matter, what work *or* course of study would you choose to be doing for the sheer enjoyment and satisfaction of doing it?**

These questions can be truly life changing. This does not mean you will necessary have a sudden and profound realisation that you should be doing something completely different (although you might!) – what it will allow you to do is to recognise how much time you are or are not spending pursuing what is important to you.

Career Development

To explore our working life (or if you are currently not working, focus on what will be important to you when, and if, you return to work), it is helpful to begin by considering what needs are (or are not) currently being met.

Imagine now, for the purpose of the following exercise, that you can tailor a job specifically to your needs and abilities.

Exercise 5/2

Write a list that covers all of your needs in relation to each of the areas below. As already mentioned, we really do tend to get what we focus on, so ensure that you state everything in the positive (for example, rather than 'I don't want to be taken for granted' say 'It is important my contribution is appreciated'):

- Financial (security, freedom, independence)
- Social (fun, teamwork, social life)
- Emotional (recognition, praise, sense of self-worth)
- Professional (trainings, certifications, opportunities).

When you have completed this list, take time to put the points in order of importance. These are your 'career values' and it would be useful to think now about how well your current working life is meeting those needs.

Exercise 6/2

Now take time to consider these questions:

- When talking to your friends or partner about your work, is there anything you repeatedly complain about?

- Do you feel you are fairly paid (or are able to pay yourself) for the hours that you work and the work that you do?

- **Do you have time to do all that you need to do every day, or do you always feel you have too much to achieve in the time you have?**

- **Do you enjoy working with your colleagues, customers or clients and feel they appreciate you?**

- **Do you feel your work allows you to develop your skills practically and professionally?**

- **What do you find most challenging or frustrating about your work?**

- **What else would you ideally like to get from your work if you could have anything?**

If there are things that are making us unhappy in any area of our lives, it is crucial to question our part, however small, in creating the situation. In order to make any positive changes in our lives we need to recognise what we, ourselves, can do to bring those changes about.

Exercise 7/2:

- **Do you feel you are motivated and committed to doing the work you do to the best of your ability?**

- **Are you working in an efficient and organised way, or would you benefit from taking the time to focus on doing that?**

- **Is there anything you have to do in your working day that you do not feel totally capable of doing?**

- **Do you need further training in order to do your job well and, if so, have you taken action to put that in place?**

• How do you think your colleagues perceive you; do they see you as helpful, capable and a good team player?

If we have a colleague (or a boss) who is disrespectful, unappreciative or rude to us on a regular basis, it is important to think about how we may be allowing that to happen. Think specifically about what they do or say and ask yourself what could be making them behave that way.

Try to really look through their eyes and understand what might be going on for them. Very often, if people are making our lives unpleasant, it is because they are either insecure or unhappy themselves. This does not (in any way) render unpleasant behaviour acceptable – it simply allows us to take their actions less personally and thus communicate in a more positive and empowered way. We do, however, also, of course, need to consider whether we could be doing anything to unintentionally irritate, antagonise or upset them.

Whatever the cause of unpleasant behaviour, it is important that we communicate calmly with the person doing the behaviour (rather than to everyone else). We then need to focus on the one thing we would really like that person to understand (and I mean completely understand) and hold that thought clearly in our mind when we communicate with them. If we communicate calmly, share our thoughts honestly, listen politely and take responsibility for anything we need to, we will always be giving ourselves the best chance to get a good result from the interaction. We will then, hopefully, be able to move on positively and have the respect of those around us.

Exercise 8/2

• What do you need from your current work to make you feel content, happy and appreciated if you currently do not?

• What do you need to do to make those things more likely to happen?

• Have you calmly and clearly communicated what it is you need to the right person?

• Is the work you currently do able to satisfy your career values, or should you be considering a career change?

Whilst it can feel daunting to think about retraining, it can also, ultimately, be liberating. The first thing is to recognise whether the work we do does not (and will not in the future) give us what we need. If this is the situation you are currently in, then give yourself the opportunity to consider all of your options.

To free up our thinking, it is important to initially put aside the logistical concerns when researching different careers and retraining opportunities. Only when we have done our exploring should we think about how we may be able to fit retraining into our current life situation, whether that is full or part-time, distance learning or on-the-job training.

If our current work place has the potential to give us what we need (providing certain issues were dealt with), then we need to decide on what action we need to take and make a commitment to ourselves to take it.

Personal Development

Developing ourselves, whether it is for the good of our career or for the sheer satisfaction of achieving something new, can give us tremendous purpose and pleasure in our everyday lives.

All of us can incorrectly believe that some things are beyond our ability when they are not. Whilst we need to be realistic about what we can achieve we often totally underestimate what are capable of achieving if we devoted enough time and energy to it.

This underestimation comes about through the limiting beliefs we hold about ourselves; more often than not we take these limiting beliefs on from significant adults during our childhood years when labels (wittingly or unwittingly) are bestowed upon us from our parents, our teachers and other significant adults (e.g. she is very shy/outgoing, academic/not academic, musical/not musically gifted, sporty/not a natural sportsperson, etc.). Sometimes these labels are given to us by default as one of our siblings may have already 'taken' a role (for example, if you have an exceptionally academic sibling, you may not perceive yourself at the 'clever one' even if you actually have a very high IQ!).

As children these labels are easily integrated into the very core of our being, which, unless we question their validity, can render us reluctant to take on certain new challenges.

Exercise 9/2

• What labels might you have been given when you were a child?

• Are there things you believe you would never be able to master or do?

• What evidence do you have to back up these beliefs?

Think of people you might know who, as adults, have mastered a new language, a new instrument or gained the skills to create a magnificent piece of artwork. Very often, we look on and wish we had the time, inclination and talent to do the same. Interestingly though, when we allow ourselves the time and opportunity to attempt something new, we so often surprise ourselves and uncover a wonderful new passion to enjoy.

Exercise 10/2

• What skills and abilities do you admire in others?

• If you could acquire a new skill by this time next year, what would you choose for it to be?

• Is there something that you have always wanted to master but have never even tried?

Next Steps...

Giving thought to all of the above allows you to truly take stock of where you are in your career and your personal development. It would be useful now for you to answer these goal-setting questions in light of any new awareness you may have gained from doing the previous exercises.

Exercise 11/2

Goal setting for your career and personal development:

•	**What, if anything, needs to change for you to have the working life you desire?**

•	**What action, if any, do you need to take to put those changes in place?**

•	**What new skill(s) would you like to acquire and by when?**

•	**What action, if any, do you need to take to give yourself the time to master those new skills?**

Finally, we should all allow our 'inner teenager' to ponder on the meaning of life and our purpose on this planet. As adults we can all get so focused on getting through our everyday tasks, meeting our commitments and paying our bills, that we can forget to step back and look at what we want to achieve for ourselves. When we are teenagers we dare to dream; when we are adults we can take steps to make those dreams our reality.

As the great Thomas Edison once said:

'If we did all the things we were capable of, we would literally astound ourselves'

CHAPTER 3

FAMILY

In this chapter we will be looking at our roles in our family; as a daughter, a sister and (if you have children) as a mother. We will also be looking at how well our relationships are working with our parents, our siblings and our children; what is currently running smoothly, what could be running even better and what steps we can take if there are things we'd like to change.

Firstly let's look at the main role you play in your family. This may be a role you have actively sought or it may be a role that has evolved through the particular dynamics of your family. As you read through the roles below you may feel that, at different times, you play them all. What we are looking to identify is the role that resonates with you the most.

The Matriarch

This woman is effectively the head of the family (or, traditionally, the tribe). She diaries family gatherings, ensures family celebrations are organised and is always there in a crisis. Some women adopt this role very early on in their lives, especially if their mother is absent or vulnerable in any way. Many women, however, take this role on when they become mothers themselves as the new sense of responsibility they feel towards their child can expand to the functioning of the wider family unit. It is important, however, that The Matriarch sometimes lets other family members take responsibility for things so as to ensure that she has enough time to care for herself and her own needs.

The Dependent

This is the woman who holds onto her 'child' status whenever she is allowed to; she carries an expectation that other family members will look after her with whatever help she might need. The dependent does not tend to organise family functions or celebrations, instead expecting that others will do this for her. The dependent will not hesitate to ask for help with financial, practical or emotional issues but rarely notices if other family members need support. If she did realise, she would, most likely, feel unable to provide it. It is important that The Dependent learns how to tap into her own inner strength in order to feel empowered enough to take charge of her own destiny.

The Martyr

This is the person who feels life is very hard; she can feel put upon by her family and, although she may do a lot for those around her, will do so with an air of weariness or even resentment. The Martyr tends to put everyone's needs before her own, resulting in her feeling she has very little time, help or support for herself. She may complain about this but tends not to ask for help from others in any meaningful or productive way. It is important that The Martyr takes time to re-evaluate her boundaries and expectations and learns how to communicate them to those around her in an assertive and positive manner in order that she can get balance back in her life and let go of feeling exhausted and resentful.

The Mediator

This is the person who is forever sorting out family disputes or disagreements; soothing ruffled feathers, suggesting compromises and ensuring everyone is all right. She tends to be the one to whom everyone turns if they are having problems and is known as being a great listener. She can sometimes feel her own needs or problems can go unrecognised by those around her. It is important that The Mediator learns to have clear boundaries around when (and how) she is willing to support other family members and, in addition, would benefit from learning how to ask for support when she needs it herself.

The Connected

This person can slip between roles with ease depending on the situation she finds herself in. She is happy to organise family functions if needs be, although she is equally happy to just do her part in putting together a celebration should someone else in the family be organising it. She enjoys her family and maintains good contact with members, remembering birthdays and important events. She feels able to ask for support from family members when she needs it, although is also very able and willing to step in to support others when necessary.

It is useful to have a real awareness of the roles we have in our family so that (should we feel we need to) we can choose to take on a different role.

Exercise 1/3:

•　　**What role(s) do you have in your family most of the time?**

•　　**What key changes, if any, would you like to make in order to have the role(s) you would like to have in your family?**

•　　**How would your family react if you started acting in this way?**

•　　**What difference, if any, would it make to your life in practical terms?**

•　　**What difference, if any, would it make to your feelings about yourself?**

As discussed in the first chapter of this book (on intimate relationships) it is incredibly empowering to think of every relationship we have as a well-choreographed dance. If we wish to change how the relationship is running we must first think about changing our side of the dance. That way, the other person has to change their behaviour in order to keep dancing.

In light of that, we are now going to look at the specific relationships we have in our family.

Blame it on the parents?

Our relationships with our parents are the most influential we have during our formative years and, very often, beyond. Whilst each of us is born with our own biologically rooted individual differences that create tendencies for us to behave in particular ways, our parents, because of their own temperaments and their own experiences, will respond to our needs in a particular way.

As any parent of more than one child knows, each of their children evokes different feelings in them and provokes different reactions. This goes some way to explaining why our personal relationship with our parents (whatever that is) may differ so much from the relationship our brothers or sisters may have with them.

During childhood we literally learn how to 'be' in the world from the significant adults around us. We take on board labels and limiting beliefs handed out to us unwittingly, which (unless we question them and seek evidence to the contrary) will shape us as individuals. In addition, we learn how to 'do' relationships; how to be a sister, a wife and a mother, by literally 'modelling' what we see. As children we do this unconsciously, which is why, *even* when we do not like a particular behaviour, we will often catch ourselves repeating it.

It is easy to blame our parents for difficulties we experienced as a child or even, perhaps, difficulties we have now. It is, however, important to recognise that parents 'parent' in the best way they can; they do what they believe to be right based on their own understandings and experiences. Recognising this can allow us to reflect on our relationships with our parents from a more insightful position.

It would be useful to now think about the relationship you had with your parents as a child as you complete the next exercise.

Exercise 2/3

• **What did you love and admire about each of your parents as you were growing up?**

• **What did you find hardest about each of them?**

• **What values and beliefs have you taken from your parents?**

• **What was the most important thing each of them taught you as you were growing up?**

In addition to reflecting on our childhood relationship with our parents, it is also important to reflect on how our relationship is now. As we grow, and move into adulthood, the way we interact with our parents naturally changes and evolves; the power relationship equals out as we become less reliant upon them emotionally and financially. As we all know, however, very often the hardest criticism to take can still be that (intentional or not) handed out by our parents. Think now about the dance you dance with your parents as an adult.

Exercise 3/3

• What do you enjoy (or cherish) about spending time with your parent(s) now?

• What is the best way for you to spend time with your parent(s)?

• What do you sometimes find frustrating about your parents now?

• Is there anything you feel your parents don't know or understand about you that you would like them to?

• Is there anything you would like to understand more about your parents?

As we, ourselves, get older, we can find ourselves becoming more concerned with our parents' well-being and, as women, we can be very quick to take on the role of nurturer or carer. If this role evolves through sudden necessity without any real thought as to what we can manage, then it can come hand in hand with the negative feelings of guilt (for not doing 'enough') or possible resentment (for doing 'too much'). If you are in this position I urge you to take time with the next exercise.

Exercise 4/3

• What support do your parent(s) need both emotionally and practically?

• What support can you reasonably offer and are happy to give on a regular basis?

- **If you have siblings, are they doing their part in supporting your parents and, if not, why not?**

- **What other options are there for your parent(s) and you to have the support they need and for you to maintain a healthy relationship with them?**

If everything follows the natural order of things, our parents will leave this planet before we do and we will experience a world without them. This harsh reality, however, should not stop us from ensuring that our relationship with our parents, even when elderly, is the best it can be through honest and open communication and a mutual understanding of one another's needs.

Brothers & Sisters

Our siblings hold a privileged position in our lives; they have shared a huge part of our journey with us and knew us before we became our polished (or not so polished!) adult selves.

We can (and usually do) differ in temperament hugely from our siblings and yet there will, at our core, always be the common ground and shared understandings that come from growing up with the same parents, sleeping under the same roof and eating at the same table.

The family roles we take on can be most clearly seen between siblings because, as children, each of us vies for our own unique position within a family. Siblings do not hesitate to label one another (the happy/moody one, the goody two-shoes/naughty one, the sensible/crazy one etc.) and these labels really can become part of who we are.

Exercise 5/3

- What positive labels were you given by your sibling(s)?
- What negative labels were you given by your sibling(s)?
- What did you enjoy doing with each of your sibling(s) when you were growing up?
- What did you find frustrating about each of your sibling(s) when you were growing up?
- What labels did you bestow upon *them*?

When we think about these questions we inevitably look back through our childhood lenses and will remember how it was to be a child in our family. Those of us who grew up with siblings had the benefit of being able to learn very early on how to handle peer relations; we had to compete with them, wrestle with feelings of jealousy and master the art of negotiation. In addition, if we are lucky, they also allowed us to experience the joy of companionship from a very early age. In short, our siblings help us to understand ourselves and others. If the relationship is strong as adults, they can continue to do so.

Exercise 6/3

- What do you love and admire about each of your sibling(s) and who they have become?
- Has anything surprised you about the way they are as an adult?

- **What, if anything, do you find hard about your relationship?**

- **What, if anything, do you think each of your siblings might find hard in their relationship with you?**

- **What changes, if any, would you need to make if you wanted your relationship with your sibling(s) to feel more mutually supportive and connected?**

Our children

Our children can be the source of our greatest happiness, our greatest pride and our greatest anxiety. When we have our first child we are plunged into an emotionally heightened world that is never quite the same. As mothers, we have to juggle our own needs with those of our children; we are keyed into their moods, their challenges and, as they grow, their dreams. In addition, as we all know, there are very real, day-to-day practicalities that mean we can sometimes forget the big picture of how we want to 'be' as a parent and what type of relationship we ultimately want to have with our children. The following exercise will help you to key into your parenting values.

Exercise 7/3

- **What do you really love about being a parent?**

- **What do you find hardest about being a parent?**

- **What are the things you sometimes find yourself repeating from your own experience of being parented?**

- **What values do you most want to pass on to your child?**

- **When you imagine your child as an adult, what would you most like them to say about how you were as a parent to them while they were growing up?**

None of us can be a perfect parent (and we all know such a thing does not exist), however, what we can all strive for, is to be the best parent we can be. Positive parenting comes from giving our child unconditional love that is coupled with clearly communicated and consistently reinforced boundaries.

Much of a child's understanding of who they are and how much they are loved and appreciated comes from the significant adults in their lives; pointing out the things we love about our child is a wonderful way of providing them with positive labels to live up to. Crucially, children will always do their best to live up to the labels we, as parents, give them (whether they are positive or negative).

Exercise 8/3

- **What do you really love and admire about your child (or each of your children) as a person?**
- **What is wonderful about having them as your son or daughter?**
- **When was the last time you told them how special they are to you?**

If you are feeling in anyway 'disconnected' from your child the quickest way to reconnect is to commit to spending some one-to-one time with them; doing something you *both* enjoy so that you can 're-bond'. This does not have to be an amazing day out, rather it is more helpful to think about activities you can commit to doing together at least once a week, such as painting, baking or playing a board game. For older children, committing to giving them regular time to talk or share a trip to a coffee shop can be a wonderful way to reconnect and provide a perfect opportunity to get back into their world.

Exercise 9/3

• **How connected do you feel to your child (or each of your children) at the moment?**

• **What do you and your child (or each of your children) most enjoy doing together?**

• **When did you last spend some one-to-one time with your child (or each of your children)?**

• **If they are teenagers, how much do you feel you know about what is going on for your child (or each of your children) right now?**

In order to flourish, as well as feeling loved, children also need to know not only what is expected of them, but also what they can expect from us in return. The best way to achieve this is through ensuring we have clear and consistently reinforced boundaries around unacceptable behaviours.

Many of us struggle with this and yet putting clear boundaries and consequences in place is much easier than most of us realise.

An important note...

We do need to ensure that we don't unwittingly give our children negative labels when putting our boundaries in place. We do this by always talking about what *behaviours* are unacceptable, rather than saying what is unacceptable *about them*. For example, it is completely fine to say 'that *behaviour* is selfish', however, it is very unhelpful to say *'you* are so selfish'. We all know we can chose to change our behaviour, however, if we believe we do something because of who we are, we tend to feel utterly powerless to change it. Our children feel this most acutely because, as we have seen, they do not tend to question the labels we give them.

Importantly, if you are reading this worrying that you may have given your child any negative 'labels', the key now is to pay attention to (even the slightest) behaviour that demonstrates the opposite behaviour so that you can effectively 're-label' them. For example, if you feel you have 'labelled' your child as 'disorganised', the minute they do something *remotely* organised, all you need to do is say 'I have really noticed that you are *becoming* so organised'. This is a hypnotic language pattern that allows you to swiftly change their belief system and give them something totally empowering to live up to.

The following exercise will allow you to really reflect on what boundaries and consequences would most help you to feel back in control if you do not currently feel you are.

Exercise 10/3

• **Do you have clear routines that allow your child (or children) to know exactly what is expected of them at crucial times of the day?**

- **What are your 'buttons'; the behaviours that drive you crazy?**

- **How good are you at explaining clearly and specifically, what behaviours are unacceptable to you and why?**

- **What consequences have you put in place to support those boundaries?**

- **Have you taken time to clearly explain the consequences to your child?**

- **How consistent are you at ensuring those consequences are enforced *every* time your child goes through a boundary?**

Putting routines and boundaries firmly in place immediately allows us to feel calmer, more in control and more able to enjoy and appreciate our children. Even with our children we dance a certain (sometimes unhelpful) dance, so taking time to think about the patterns of behaviour we repeat and deciding what needs to change allows us to create a happier home life for everyone including ourselves.

Next Steps...

Having taken stock of where you are with your family and your roles within it; as a daughter, a sister and a mother, you are now in a great position to set yourself some clear and attainable goals for the future.

Exercise 11/3

Goal setting questions for your family:

- **What role(s) do you want to have in your family?**
- **What changes, if any, do you need to make to have the best possible relationships with your parent(s)?**
- **What changes, if any, do you need to make to enjoy your relationships with your sibling(s) even more?**
- **What changes, if any, do you need to make for you to be the parent you want to be?**

They say we choose our friends, not our family, but what we can do is choose for it to be the best it can be.

As Jane Howard, the American writer, once said:

'Call it a clan, call it a network, call it a tribe, call it a family. Whatever you call it, whoever you are, you need one.'

CHAPTER 4

PHYSICAL WELL-BEING

In this chapter we will be taking stock of our physical well-being; we will explore what steps we need to take to enable us to feel stronger, more energized and more positive about our bodies, both inside and out.

When we think of our physical well-being, many of us focus on our external appearance and forget to tune into our *inner* health and well-being. Therefore, wherever you are (and whatever you are doing right now) I would like you to take five minutes to sit quietly and really listen to (and focus on) your own, *amazing* body as you consider the questions in the exercise below. As you do so, ensure you are breathing slowly and deeply, allowing your tummy to gently move outwards as you inhale and inwards as you exhale.

Exercise 1/4

- **Do you have any aches or pains you have been ignoring?**
- **Do you feel relaxed or stressed?**

- **Do you feel well-rested or tired?**

- **How well are you currently looking after yourself and your body?**

- **If you are neglecting to look after yourself and your body, how is that making you feel *right now*?**

As women, we can be so focused on what we don't like about our bodies that we forget to appreciate what our bodies do for us. Our bodies, when healthy, allow us to walk, run, swim, ski, cycle, horse ride, make love, dance and many things besides. If we focus solely on our 'faults' we can forget to appreciate all that is amazing about our bodies. Importantly, if we take a solely critical stance, it is impossible to truly nurture and care for ourselves.

Exercise 2/4

- **How kind are you to yourself when you look in the mirror?**

- **What do you like about your face and your body?**

- **What do you appreciate about your body for what it allows you to do and to enjoy in life?**

We will now explore all of the ways in which we need to care for our physical well-being in order for you to be able to review how well you are looking after yourself right now.

Health checks

As women we tend to be very good at ensuring those in our care have regular dental, orthodontist or hygienist checks and, if they need to visit a doctor or a specialist, we will make it happen. We tend *not* to be so good at ensuring that we have regular dental and health checks for ourselves.

Exercise 3/4

• **Is there anything worrying you about your health for which you have not yet made an appointment to get checked out?**

• **Do you regularly see your dentist, and is there any extra dental work that you have always wanted to have done but have never got round to?**

• **Are you up to date with all of your well woman screening tests?**

Taking time to focus on our health in the same way we do for those in our care can (literally) be a lifesaver. If you are not currently good at prioritising your needs, remind yourself that if you do not take care of yourself you are at risk of rendering yourself incapable of caring for others.

It occurred to me many years ago when sitting on a plane with my children, that the safety procedures provide a wonderful analogy for life; we are told, in the event of an emergency, to put our own oxygen masks on *before* we attend to the needs of anyone in our care thus ensuring we are in a position to do so. In order for any of us to successfully care for others, we absolutely *must* take care of ourselves, and our needs, first.

Stress and Anxiety

Research now clearly shows that stress and anxiety affect not only how we feel, think and behave, they *also* affect how our bodies work. We will all, inevitably, have some stressful times in our lives; times when we feel we are under so much mental or emotional pressure that we subsequently feel overwhelmed and out of control of our lives. We will also *all* have times when we feel anxious. It is useful to understand the difference between stress and anxiety because, although they can feel quite similar, they have very different causes. While stress is caused by the reality of having too much to cope with in our lives at any one time, anxiety is caused by imagined scenarios of situations of events that may go wrong.

When we are stressed or anxious our body releases the hormone and neurotransmitter Epinephrine (also known as adrenaline). A small burst of adrenaline can actually be useful (increasing activity, motivation and focus), however, living in a state of constant stress or anxiety and the perpetually raised adrenaline levels that accompany those feelings, can have serious effects on our health.

If you are currently feeling stressed or anxious give yourself time to complete the following exercise.

Exercise 4/4

- **What are you currently worrying about most in life?**

- **Are you able to, at times, switch off from your current concerns and, if so, what activity or pastime allows you to do that?**

- **Do you often tell yourself that you will be less stressed when something happens (e.g. when you have got through this busy month, got the salary raise you need, completed a particular project etc.)?**

- **If you knew this was your last year on the planet, which of the things you are currently stressed or anxious about about would still cause you concern?**

Once we understand what causes us stress and are honest about what we are 'waiting' for in order for it to pass, we are in a good position to re-evaluate the choices we are currently making. There are times when we, genuinely, do need to complete something in order for our stress to be relieved. If this is over a long period of time, however, it becomes a very unhealthy way to live. In addition, we often mistakenly believe we simply need to do *more* in order to cope with things better, when the reality is we actually need to do *less* or we need to do things *differently*.

Exercise 5/4

- **If your stress comes from feeling you never have enough time, what can you either stop doing or delegate to someone else?**

- **If your stress comes from finding something too difficult, what support do you need to be able to either do it or to let go of it?**

- **If your stress comes from feeling financially vulnerable, consider what would need to happen for you to feel financially secure?**

- **Do you currently have things in your life that cost you money that you would consider letting go of in exchange for having a less stressful life?**

- **If your stress comes from something you simply cannot control, what are your options if things don't work out the way you want them to?**

When we acknowledge the things we cannot change, it frees us up to focus on the things we can. If we cannot alter, or influence, the outcome of something we are feeling stressed about, the best thing for us to do is to focus on what our options are if things don't work out the way we'd like.

In addition, when we are feeling stressed, we very often forget to nurture and care for ourselves, simply adding to our feeling that our life is out of control. If we stop and review our routine and start doing small, kind things for ourselves every day we immediately feel calmer and happier.

Sleep

All of us function better when we are well-rested; waking up feeling refreshed allows us all to not only *manage* more of what we wish to during the day but also to *enjoy* what we are doing. In addition, sleep is essential for healthy cell growth and for cell and tissue repair.

If you feel exhausted a lot of the time, it is really good to think about what needs to change in order for you to feel rested.

Exercise 6/4

- How do you feel when you wake up most mornings?
- Do you manage to go to bed at the time you plan to most evenings?
- Do you prepare yourself for a good night's sleep by having 'down time' (without computers or phones) before bed?
- What, if anything, do you need to do to improve your sleeping habits?
- If you are currently not getting enough sleep, how would it feel to wake up every day bursting with energy and what difference would that make to your life?

Regular exercise

In addition to getting enough sleep, it is important to take stock of our fitness levels. When we are not at our fittest we can feel we have such a huge mountain to climb that we lose sight of the fact that small changes to our routine can increase our fitness levels significantly and get us to the first plateau.

A crucial factor in whether we stick to a new exercise regime or not is whether we enjoy (or at least bear!) the activity we have chosen to do. Attending the gym three days a week is perfect if you are a natural (even if lapsed) gym bunny. However, if pounding on a treadmill is your personal idea of hell, it is *never* going to be sustainable. To understand the best way for *you* to exercise, it is important to really understand yourself.

Exercise 7/4

• **When you were a child, what different sports and activities did you gravitate towards?**

• **Did they tend to be competitive or were they just for the fun of taking part?**

• **Is it important for you to be with others (e.g. attending a fitness class, playing tennis with a friend) or are you happier doing things alone (e.g. power walking, riding, cycling)?**

Picking the right type of exercise *and* adjusting our routine to allow for it, allows us to incorporate exercise into our life in a sustainable way, enabling us to feel, ultimately, fitter, more toned, and more energised. The great thing is that if we persevere, then over time, the exercise we have chosen to do gets increasingly easier and we naturally step up to do more. Remember then, if you do not currently do much, it really is just about taking those first small steps and a toned and healthy body will, in time, be yours.

Eating habits

Research shows there are (sadly) very few women who have an entirely healthy relationship with food. We call certain foods 'bad' and feel 'naughty' if we make the 'wrong' choices, we try to be 'good' and chastise ourselves if we aren't.

We treat the scales as revered, all-knowing, all-powerful dictators of happiness; if our weight is where we want it to be we can bounce off with a spring in our step, if it isn't we can feel despondent and weak. Luckily, for many, this moment passes quite quickly, but for some, the scales can set the tone for the entire day.

If this describes you then I would urge you to make a shift in your thinking which will allow you to be freer and happier. The healthiest way to think about food is that it is our fuel; we need calories to live and we need calories to function.

In the Western world we are lucky enough to be able to choose from a wide range of food fuels. We can choose poor quality, cheap fuel that allows us initially to go faster but then (if used too much over time) clogs up our engines making them sluggish and corroded. Alternatively, we can choose quality fuel that allows us to glide smoothly at the speeds we choose with a well-oiled and smooth running engine beneath us.

It is important to recognise that a little bit of the poor fuel won't hurt us (in fact, there are times when we actually benefit from the boost it can give us) but it is, as we all know, about balance.

Having *mainly* quality fuel made up of good quality protein, high fibre carbohydrates and plenty of fruit and vegetables, allows our engine to purr.

Despite the current economic climate, the diet industry in the UK continues to thrive. Every week there are new ideas about *what* we should or shouldn't eat and *when* we should or shouldn't eat it. The reality is that each and every one of us knows *exactly* how to lose weight; we simply need to eat fewer calories than we actually use. So, if you do wish to lose weight (or just improve your diet), it is helpful to look within to what you know works for you, and then make adjustments in a planned and proactive way so that it becomes not only easily 'doable', it also becomes a way of caring for yourself.

Exercise 8/4

• **What is your ideal weight taking into account your height and build?**

• **How would it feel to be that weight now (if you are not currently that weight)?**

• **What healthy foods do you really enjoy?**

• **How good are you at thinking about what you want to eat during the week and making sure you have organised that for yourself?**

• **If you currently feel you need to lose weight, what is the way that you know works best *for you*?**

Losing weight is not rocket science; trust your own knowledge of what works for you, plan what foods you wish to eat and, *crucially*, treat yourself as important enough to shop for. This ensures you have all that you need to maintain your new healthy diet.

In addition, here are five key common sense tips for maintaining a healthy diet:

1.   No food is 'evil' and it can be really helpful to allow yourself a small treat every day (dark chocolate is particularly good as it is now well-documented that a little bit of this every day has its own health benefits).

2.   It has been shown that we consume more calories on a day when we are tired as we are more likely to crave sugar so reviewing your sleep patterns and ensuring you are well-rested, makes losing weight much easier.

3.   We also all tend to crave sugar and high fat food when we are hungry, so it can be really helpful to allow yourself high-protein, low-fat snacks during the day (e.g. a yogurt or a handful of raw nuts). This is particularly true for women; our metabolism tends to be faster when eating many small meals (or snacks) rather that three large ones.

4.   If we wish to lose weight, it is useful to avoid carbohydrates after 6pm for the simple reason we are not going to burn those calories off in our sleep. So (unless you are going out partying and dancing all night!) it's best to stick to protein and salad or vegetables in the evening.

5.   We very often confuse thirst for hunger so, if you are trying to lose weight, ensure you are well-hydrated at all times.

Just like beginning a new exercise regime, healthy eating needs to become part of our everyday routine to have an effect. After just a few weeks, new behavioural patterns simply become part of our way of being; the effort then is minimal and the rewards are huge.

Healthy hydration

The European Food Safety Authority recommends that women should drink about 1.6 litres of fluid a day (around eight 200ml glasses). When we do not drink enough fluid we are prone to headaches, lethargy and constipation. If you don't currently drink enough water, simply getting into the habit of drinking a couple of large jugs or bottles of water every day will, within weeks, make you feel noticeably more energetic and clearer headed. In addition, many (previously dehydrated) women notice a significant change in the appearance of their skin; specifically a dramatic improvement in dark circles, blotches and fine lines.

Whilst reviewing the amount of non-alcoholic fluid we drink, it is also important for us to review of the amount of alcoholic fluid we might drink. The NHS recommends that women should not regularly drink more that 2 or 3 units of alcohol a day (2 or 3 *small* glasses of wine). Drinking too much alcohol on a regular basis can cause fatigue, depression, weight gain and sleep problems (and, of course, longer term, more serious health risks). The great thing is that *as soon as* we start cutting back on alcohol, we notice some immediate benefits; we feel better in the morning, less tired during the day and tend to have clearer, brighter skin.

As with regular exercise and healthy eating, ensuring we are healthily hydrated is all about establishing great habits that become a simple everyday part of how we care for ourselves.

The best you can be: see it, hear it and feel it...

One of the most powerful techniques we can use when we want to make changes to our life is to focus on our vision of our best selves every day. So imagine now that you are already in the best physical shape you could be; all of your clothes fit perfectly, you feel energised, healthy and toned. When we allow ourselves to truly visualise this and enjoy the feelings that go with it, we set our whole system up for success.

Exercise 9/4

If your body was exactly as you wanted to be:

- **How would the world feel to you?**
- **What would you no longer have in your life?**
- **Is there anything it would allow you to do that you currently do not?**

Next steps...

You are now in a great position to take stock of where you are with regard to your physical well-being and set yourself some great goals for the future.

Exercise 10/4

Goal setting questions for your physical well-being:

•　　　What medical or dental appointments, if any, do you need to make?

•　　　What changes, if any, do you need to make to let go of the stress in your life?

•　　　What changes, if any, do you need to make to ensure you incorporate enough sleep into your life?

•　　　What changes, if any, are you going to make to incorporate enough exercise into your life?

•　　　What changes, if any, are you going to make to ensure you eat healthily in order to be at, and maintain, your ideal weight?

•　　　What changes, if any, are you going to make to ensure you are totally hydrated at all times?

•　　　What changes, if any, are you going to make to your alcohol consumption?

Taking time out to think about (and act on) our needs is about treating ourselves with respect, kindness and appreciation, which allows us to have the healthy and happy life we desire.

As Mahatma Gandhi once said:

'It is health that is real wealth and not pieces of gold and silver.'

CHAPTER 5

HOME ENVIRONMENT

In this chapter we are going to take stock of your home environment to ensure it feels like your personal sanctuary; a place you can retreat to, recharge and share special time with your loved ones.

This chapter is not about creating an immaculate home; it is about creating your space in such a way that, when you are in it, you feel relaxed and totally yourself. As you read through the chapter, therefore, I would like you to focus on the things that give *you* personal pleasure, be that a simple vase of flowers on the kitchen table, the feeling of clean sheets as you climb into bed or the perfect shady spot to sit in your garden and enjoy a book.

Before we explore how well you are using the different spaces in your home, it would be good to focus on some key questions.

Exercise 1/5

•   What do you currently love about being in your home?

•   What are you currently not happy with about your home?

•   What are the everyday chores that you never quite feel on top of?

•   Where do you carry out your admin and store your paperwork?

•   Which space(s) do you use to relax in?

In addition, it is also good to have a real awareness of the general 'feel' you like, in your home and in other people's.

Exercise 2/5

•   How much involvement did you have in choosing the decor in your home?

•   What colours do you love (bold/muted, glossy/matte, plain/contrasting)?

•   What style do you like (cottage/contemporary, kitsch/minimalistic, vintage/modern)?

•   What home furnishing shops do you love and what is it about their style that you admire?

•   Which of your friend's houses do you feel most 'at home' in and why?

Even if we are not currently refurbishing our home, it is good to have a real understanding of what we like so that, when we do need to redecorate or simply replace something (as we all inevitably do), we can move towards the look, the feel and the type of space that we want to create.

Creating 'vision' boards can be really useful in helping us to focus on *any* area of our lives, but never more so than for our home. If you wish to change the feel of your home (either now or over time), have some fun creating your own board; collecting and putting together fabrics, paint colours, pictures of rooms and home accessories that fit your desired look. Pick out the photos, colours and ideas that give you real pleasure just looking at them.

Exploring the spaces in your home

It is useful to consider how you perceive the spaces in your home, what you use them for and whether each space is working for you. We will also consider whether there are practical steps you can take to make your life feel easier and less cluttered. If you have a space that really isn't working, it can be worth taking a morning to focus purely on that area and complete the suggested tasks for that room.

Kitchen Space

Many of us see our kitchen as the heart of our home; it is the place we start the day, prepare food, talk, laugh, eat and welcome our friends in to share a drink and catch up on life. We can also see it as a place that needs constant attention to maintain any sort of order!

Exercise 3/5

• What are the different things you use your kitchen for?

• How well does the layout of your kitchen work for you?

• Would moving items to different cupboards or drawers make it more 'user-friendly'?

• Do you have items in your cupboards that you no longer use and can't imagine ever using again?

• When do you most enjoy being in your kitchen?

• Does everyone in the house help with the kitchen chores?

• Are there specific jobs you could (and should) give to other members of your household?

Re-organising and streamlining our kitchen cupboards can make it a much more ergonomically friendly. Over time we can collect a scarily large amount of devices that seem a brilliant idea at the time of purchase that we never then actually use. Re-cycling these items to people who will enjoy them can mean you no longer have to balance ten things on your lap in order to get to the bowl you really *do* need to use!

Importantly as well, in order for any of us to view our kitchen as an enjoyable place to be, it is crucial for us to feel that other members of our household help keep it tidy and clean. If you constantly feel you are the only one who does the chores, take time to talk to everyone in your house and have clear guidelines around what needs to be done and who is expected to do it.

Even those of us who do not feel we are natural domestic goddesses can enjoy cooking or baking if we have the time, the ingredients and a wonderfully clear and organised kitchen in which to operate. There is a real pleasure to be had in getting in touch with our inner Nigella and producing something to enjoy and be proud of.

Bedroom Space

Our bedrooms are our most personal of all spaces; not only is it the room where we get ready, it also tends to be the room we retreat to if we wish to be on our own to relax or recharge.

Exercise 4/5

•   **Is your bedroom a place where you can easily relax?**

•   **Does it feel uncluttered and peaceful?**

•   **Is your bed comfortable?**

•   **Are your cupboards organised and your clothes easily accessible?**

•   **Do you have a clear place with a seat and a mirror where you can get ready for your day or evening ahead?**

For some reason, even those of us who don't hoard in other areas of our lives, can hoard in our bedroom. We keep shoes we don't wear, make-up we don't use and clothes we don't like. Imagine for a moment opening your wardrobe and seeing only clothes hanging there that you know fit you, suit you and are relevant to your life.

The truth is that if we haven't worn an item in twelve months (i.e. through all the seasons) the chance of us ever wearing it again is very, very low. If you need a clear out, it can be incredibly helpful (and fun) to invite a girlfriend over, sit her down and ask for her honest opinion about the clothes you are hanging onto. You can then box up the rejects and take them to your local charity shop or sell them on eBay. If that is too hard or too painful, put the box in the garage for a six-month 'stay of execution' and see if you go out to retrieve any of the items!

Having clutter-free cupboards and drawers makes getting ready a pleasure, as does having a clutter-free space to sit at and get ready. Be tough with yourself so that your room really can feel like the haven it should be.

Bathroom Space

However small (or big) your bathroom is, it is effectively your home spa; the space you can use to wash, rejuvenate and pamper yourself.

Exercise 5/5

• **Is your bathroom cluttered with bottles, potions and creams?**

• **Could you create an easily accessible storage space so that you can have the sides and floor reasonably clear if they aren't already?**

• **Is your bathroom a place where you can easily relax and nurture yourself?**

- **Do you have scented candles so that, should you wish to, you can have a gorgeous candle lit bath?**

Our bathrooms clearly have to be functional, however, they can be so much more than just the place we wash. There are few (inexpensive) pleasures as enjoyable as the feeling of an invigorating shower or a soak in the bath, especially if the room we are in is beautifully decorated and organised.

If you do not have everything you need to be able to create a 'spa experience' in your bathroom, take time to list what you are missing (e.g. storage boxes, scented candles, soft white bath towels) and value yourself enough to treat yourself to those things next time you are able to.

Living Space

Let's think now about the area we have our 'down time'; the place we go to read, watch television, enjoy a movie or relax with our special people.

Exercise 6/5

- **What, if anything, do you love about your living space?**

- **Are you able to be in this space without feeling you are surrounded by things you 'should' be doing, repairing or completing?**

- **If you have young children, do you have toys littered around the floor?**

For our sitting rooms to be relaxing they need to be totally free of reminders of unfinished tasks, which includes not being surrounded by mess from the day. For those of you with young children, it is really worthwhile investing in a decent-sized toy box in which everything can be hidden before the evening 'child-free' time begins.

In order for our living room to be a space where we can truly wind down and relax it needs to be totally comfortable and utterly 'job-free'.

Office Space

One of the greatest weights we can all carry at home is the feeling we have dull, or overdue, paperwork hanging over us which needs completing.

Creating a space where we can easily find everything we need to do our banking, form-filling, bill-paying, flight-booking and tax returns can make these tasks far less arduous. This is especially true if we actually schedule in admin time each week, rather than expecting to somehow shoehorn it in around everything else we have going on in our lives.

Exercise 7/5

• **What are the admin jobs that you hate doing?**

• **Do you allocate time each week in which you can complete your paperwork?**

• **Do you have a clear, uncluttered desk where you can work?**

With allocated time and a well-organised space (plus a cup of tea or coffee!), it can actually be quite satisfying to sit down and clear your inbox. In addition to a clear desk (with a fully stocked drawer containing stationary and stamps) it is important to have well-organised, clearly-labelled files, so that we can lay our hands on anything we need with ease.

Spending a morning purchasing new stationary and files, shredding old paperwork, organising our office and scheduling in a regular weekly admin time allows us to approach our office space in a positive and productive state of mind.

Outside Space

Our gardens do not have to be huge (or RHS standard) for us to be able to enjoy being in them; sitting in the garden looking at a freshly mown lawn and beds bursting with flowers is one of life's simple pleasures, as is sitting in the garden enjoying a drink or a meal with friends.

Exercise 8/5

- **What do you mainly use your garden for?**
- **What do you love about your garden?**
- **What is not currently working well in your garden?**
- **Where do you sit on a sunny day in your garden?**
- **What flowers and colours give *you* special pleasure?**

• **Do you have lighting set up in your garden so you can enjoy it in the evening?**

Whilst it takes time to create the garden we want, it's also incredibly rewarding. Visiting beautiful gardens and garden centres for inspiration and taking the time to plan specific areas where we can sit in the sun, relax in the shade, dine al fresco or simply enjoy smelling the roses, means we are taking the time to create something that will give us pleasure for years. If you are in the process of creating your garden, remember that whilst waiting for seeds to take, plants to mature and buds to open, it is relatively easy to add some beautiful perennials to our beds and create pots bursting with colour and fragrance.

Next Steps...

As in all other areas of our lives, visualising what we want and how we want things to be sets up our whole system to achieve it, so now imagine walking around your well-ordered house with a cup of coffee in your hand feeling your home is just as you want it to be; you have clearly defined spaces to eat, to work and to relax. Imagine what you would see, hear and feel and what special touches you would have added to make it just as you want it to be.

Exercise 9/5

Goal setting questions for your home environment

• **Which rooms need your attention in order to make your home feel as you want it to?**

- **What equipment do you need to get in order to feel more organised and in control?**

- **What time do you need to schedule in to put these changes in place and create your special spaces, just as you want them to be?**

We can all feel we haven't got time to get our home in order, but it is truly worth prioritising the time so that your home really is your own personal sanctuary; a special place where *you* can be *you*.

As Maya Angelou once said:

'The ache for home lives in all of us, the safe place where we can go as we are and not be questioned.'

CHAPTER 6

FRIENDSHIPS

In this final chapter we will be exploring one of the most important areas of our lives, our friendships. As humans, we are fundamentally social creatures; we are all, at some level, driven by a need to love and be loved in return. This need extends beyond our intimate relationship and families, to the need to have peers who we can relate to, confide in and share experiences with.

Most of us have different friends who bring different things to our lives. It is wonderful to have friends we have known for years with whom we have experienced different phases of our lives and with whom we can enjoy the mutual understanding our shared history brings. It is also wonderful, as we move through life, to make new friends; people who can open us up to new experiences, new understandings and new ways of being.

Exercise 1/6

• **What qualities are important to you in your friends?**

- **How do you most like to spend time with each of your special friends?**

- **Do you feel you spend enough time doing those things?**

Close friends really do give us something our partners and families aren't able to; they give us the freedom to discuss issues and dilemmas without the restrictions that can be imposed by familial expectations, possessiveness or fear of change.

As we all know, it is only possible to successfully nurture a handful of truly close friends; if we try to maintain too many close friendships, we can end up spreading ourselves too thinly. Take a moment now to think about who your closest friends are, the people who make up your personal 'inner circle' and consider whether you feel able to give each of them the time and energy you would like to.

Now, think now about your friends in the next circle out. These will be people you enjoy spending time with but whom you would not necessarily think to call up with exciting news or call upon in a crisis. Consider whether there is anyone who is in *this* category who regularly demands *too* much of your time?

If you have many different friends it is useful to give thought as to where they sit for you; the more friends we have, the more we need to be proactive in organising our time so as to ensure we put enough energy into the relationships that mean the most to us in order that we can truly nurture and support those we love.

To have a friend...

Let's turn our attention now to how you, yourself, are as a friend.

Exercise 2/6

• **What do you feel one friend should provide for another?**

• **What do you like about how you are as a friend?**

• **What, if anything, do you feel you could do to be an *even* better friend?**

As well as friends providing us with wonderful companionship, friendships also need to also be mutually trusting and supportive. All of us will have times in our lives when we need to lean on our friends, and similarly, times when they will need to lean on us.

For most of us, being able to comfort and support our friends allows us to feel needed and valued. Listening, providing reassurance and talking things through, is a bonding and fulfilling part of any relationship. It is, however, equally important for us to allow ourselves to be supported by our friends.

Some of us can feel vulnerable and exposed if we share our issues with others and this can make us reluctant to let our friends comfort and support us. Not only is this a loss for ourselves, it can also result in our friends feeling shut out and excluded from our lives.

Conversely, it is equally important to recognise if we (or, indeed, one of our friends) are always in 'crisis' mode. In particular, it is important to recognise if we are always in crisis over the same issue but never take any action to change it. If this is the case, for the good of our friendships (and for our own happiness) we need to recognise the need to either accept the situation as it is or, even better, take steps towards changing it in order to move forward positively.

Exercise 3/6

• **Are you comfortable discussing your issues or upsets with your very close friends?**

• **Have you ever shut out a close friend from an issue because you chose to cope alone?**

• **Do you feel you are always in 'crisis' mode (i.e. always in need of support)?**

• **Which of your friendships are equally and mutually supportive?**

The roles we take on

All of us take on 'roles' with our friends; interestingly we can take on different roles with different people depending on how we 'fit' with them. As you read through the roles below, therefore, consider what type of roles you take on in your friendships, as well as considering what type of roles your friends take on with you.

The Queen Bee

This is the woman who feels her opinion should matter more than anyone else's; she likes to dominate the group she is part of (particularly the women in a mixed group). The Queen Bee tends to prefer the company of men and can feel threatened by any new women who join the group she is part of. To maintain her position she will, initially, be very friendly towards a new woman who joins the group but will, after establishing the relationship, begin to be judgmental and critical of her. The only women The Queen Bee feels comfortable with is those who she sees as less worthy than her in some way and those who are deferential to her. The Queen Bee would benefit from working on her own insecurities so that she can learn the pleasure that comes from having true female friends.

The Disorganised

This is the friend who has a tendency to let people down. Despite caring about her friends, she can forget important life events and challenges her friends are facing. Whilst this can, at times, be hurtful, it actually reflects a lack of routine and organisation in her own life rather than a lack of care towards her friends. The Disorganised friend tends to pull out of things last minute and holds an expectation that others will fit in with her to accommodate her, often chaotic, schedule. The Disorganised friend would benefit from taking time out to review how she is currently running her life, in order to feel more in control, less stressed and free to be the friend she truly wants to be.

The Advisor

This is the friend who always feels the need to advise her friends on the best course of action when they are facing an issue. The Advisor has a genuine desire to help people but also, very often, also has a need to control her friends (particularly those she cares about). The Advisor can also become frustrated if her friends choose not to act upon her advice. Ultimately, she often feels all she ever does is give to (and support) others when, in reality, she actively adopts this role and rarely chooses to lean on others. The challenge for the advisor is to let go of the need to manage her friends' problems, learning instead to actively listen and talk things through. It is also important for The Advisor to recognise that, in choosing not to discuss her own issues, she is denying herself the opportunity to be supported by those who love her.

The Child

This is the woman who fits well with The Advisor as The Child always asks for guidance; she feels the need to check her behaviour with others, looks for reassurance that she is doing the right thing and finds it hard to make decisions on her own. Instead of being autonomous, The Child tends to hand over her power by being overly apologetic if she does not follow her friend's advice (or even sometimes withholds information for fear of being reprimanded) and by being overly critical of herself if she makes any mistakes. The Child needs to learn to trust herself, listen to her own (inner) voice and realise that her life choices are entirely her own.

The Constant

This is the type of friend a person can truly rely upon; she will have an awareness of her friends as she goes about her life, knowing what is going on for them during any particular week. The Constant has mutually respectful, non-judgmental friendships where she is not only supportive but also comfortable being supported. She will be there to celebrate her friend's successes, as well as supporting them through life's inevitable challenges. She will let her friend's know, clearly and honestly, what she is feeling at any given time. The Constant brings much joy, support and warmth to her friends' lives.

When reviewing the roles you take on in your friends' lives (as well as the roles your friends take on with you) it is important to recognise that each of us can choose to take on a different role simply by shifting our understanding of how we truly want to be as a friend. Just as important is having a clear understanding of how we expect our friends to treat us in return.

Boundaries

As we have seen, understanding our boundaries is crucial in all of our relationships and this is no less true with friends. We are going to look now at how well you understand your friendship boundaries and whether you value yourself (and your friendships) enough to let someone know if they have hurt or upset you.

Exercise 4/6

- How do you expect to be treated by your friends?

- What behaviours would you find unacceptable from a friend?

- Can you remember a time when you have felt hurt or let down by a friend?

- How did you deal with that situation?

- Do you feel you are good at letting your friends know if they have done something you find unacceptable or hurtful?

If you feel you are not good at standing up for yourself, it is helpful to recognise that there does not have to be conflict in order for you to do so. Firstly, it is good to begin by letting our friend know how important the relationship is to us. Then, rather than focusing on what they should (or should not) have done, it is important to focus on how we are feeling (hurt, let down, disappointed etc.). The emphasis needs to be on open and honest communication and the recognition that your friendship is valuable enough to protect. If your friend is worth keeping, they will listen to what you have to say, discuss the issue and, in all likelihood, be genuinely concerned they have caused you any upset.

It is, of course, equally important for us to be able to take feedback from our friends. If we have hurt someone we care about, regardless of how aware we were (or were not) at the time, we need to apologise unreservedly for hurting them and try as hard as we can to look through their eyes and understand what they are feeling. This way we can learn from the situation and avoid making that mistake again with them, or anyone else, who is important to us.

If, despite clear communication on our part, someone continuously goes through our boundaries, it is important to consider whether that person should continue to be in our life in the way that they currently are. It can be a difficult, and upsetting, realisation that someone we have been close to is not respectful of us, or our needs. In order to be truly happy, however, we all need to value ourselves enough to walk away from anyone who does not respect us or enhance our experience of life.

If we do decide we need to have more distance from one of our friends, though, it is important to withdraw from that person with as much sensitivity and kindness as possible. Anyone who has experienced the heartache of being suddenly dropped without explanation by someone they previously felt close to, understands the pain it can cause. Withdraw gradually and, if asked, be honest enough to provide a clear explanation as to why you feel the need to look after yourself and step back.

Expanding your circles

As mentioned in the opening of this chapter, to experience life to the full, it is healthy for all of us to be receptive to welcoming new friends into our lives; meeting new people really can open our eyes to different ways of seeing and being in the world.

In addition, if you have a particular interest that no one in your friendship group shares, it is worth putting the effort into meeting someone with whom you *can* share it with. `

Exercise 5/6

• **Do you feel you have friends with whom you can do all that you wish to do?**

• **Is there an activity you previously really enjoyed doing but that is no longer part of your life?**

• **Is there an activity you have always wanted to do but have never tried due to not having someone to do it with?**

If we wish to find additional friends with similar interests the simplest way is to find out about clubs or centres where these activities are on offer and explore different ways to become involved. For some of us, it can be hard to put ourselves in new and unknown situations, but the rewards of finding people with whom we can share new, exciting and fulfilling experiences are huge.

Next Steps...

Now you are in a great position to take stock of where you are with regard to your friendships and think about setting your own personal goals to make your friendships *even* better.

Exercise 6/6

Goal setting questions for your friendships:

• What changes (if any) do you need to make to the role you currently have with each of your friends?

• Are there any friends you feel you need to be clearer with regarding your boundaries?

• Are there any friendships that no longer serve you in terms of nurturing you and supporting you?

• What friendships, if any, do you feel you need to nurture more so that they know just how important they are to you?

• In an ideal world, what would you spend more time doing with your friends and what could you do to make that happen?

Friends provide us with love and laughter; they share our pain, our joy and our dreams. We need to value ourselves enough to ensure our friendships are as positive, and as life enhancing, as they are capable of being.

As the great William Shakespeare once said:

'A friend is one that knows you as you are, understands where you have been, accepts what you have become, and still, gently allows you to grow.'

CONCLUSION

So now, at the end of our journey, it would be good to spend some time visualising how you want your life to be moving forward. We, each of us, have the ability to create the life we want; to develop ourselves so that we make the most of our unique talents and abilities, to feel physically the best we can feel, to have a home we feel totally ourselves in and have relationships with our loved ones that make us truly happy.

At any one time there can be areas of our lives that may not be running as smoothly as we'd like them to; valuing ourselves enough to work out what needs to change and putting those changes in place can be both empowering and life changing.

For all of us, change can, at times, seem daunting. However, as we know, it is only when we step outside our comfort zone (and therefore, over time, expand it) that we can positively work towards becoming all that we are capable of becoming.

When coaching a client around fear of change, I always ask them to imagine for a moment that the issue they are dealing with (the very thing that has caused them to seek help) is never going to change and they will have to deal with that problem or issue (and the emotions attached to it) for the rest of their life. For all of us, the thought of living with something that is not working *forever* can make the fear of change shrink substantially; the simple truth is, that if we do not go after what we want in life, we are unlikely ever to have it.

Let us now consider the five most common things that can hold us back from taking the steps we need to (if we let them).

1 Fear of failure

Fear of failure is one of the biggest (and most powerful) fears we can face; we can have real and understandable concerns that whatever changes we make, or attempt to make, might not work out. We may start a course that we find too hard, in terms of commitment, energy or even ability. We may apply for, or even begin, a job that we feel we can't cope with or find was not what we believed it would be. We may fail at losing the weight we want to or getting as fit as we'd like. We may put things in motion to improve our relationship only to find the relationship is not worth saving.

Whilst it is entirely possible that something *may,* indeed, not work out for us, we need to recognise that, if something is important enough to us, we *will* find another way to move towards our goal. Each and every failure we experience in life teaches us how *not* to do something; it allows us to narrow down our options and find a way forward that works. Thomas Edison, arguably one of the most prolific inventors ever to have lived, was once asked how he managed to cope with his well documented 10,000 failed attempts at inventing the light bulb before he found the solution. He answered, *'I have not failed, I just found 10,000 ways that won't work.'* Every 'failure' really does provide us with a fantastic learning opportunity.

2 Fear of being judged

All of us, to varying degrees, care about how we are perceived by the people around us. This is a necessary part of being human; we are social creatures and, as such, have a need to fit into our wider social world.

Problems occur, however, if our 'external frame of reference' (when we check our behaviours or choices are acceptable to others) becomes *more* important than our 'internal frame of reference' (when we check our behaviours or choices are acceptable to ourselves). If the balance is wrong, fear of others judging us can stop us experiencing new and exciting opportunities. The reality is that the people who love us will be there to support us and stand by us regardless of how our endeavours work out. Other people may, indeed, judge us harshly or unfairly, but if they are people who do not have our best interests at heart (or do not even really know us), we must never allow their opinions to hold us back.

3 Self-sabotage

If we struggle to ever achieve our goals *despite always making a great start towards them* it is worth considering whether we are, in fact, unwittingly carrying out some self-sabotage. This can come into play if our goal (however desirable it is to us) will, in some way, force us to face other challenges or will, somehow, unsettle us.

For example, a woman who has an unconscious fear of stepping back into the work environment after being at home, may believe that she just needs to get her cluttered house sorted and her paperwork mountain cleared before she can even *think* about the next phase of her life. However, if she does not recognise (and face) the fear she is feeling, it is likely that every time she begins making positive inroads into having a wonderfully ordered home, she will completely lose focus and come to a grinding halt. Unconsciously manufactured 'busyness' is a very common form of avoidance.

Another (surprisingly common) example is a woman who believes she wants nothing more that to lose weight and get fit but unconsciously fears that, in doing so, she may then have to deal with re-evaluating her relationship, her sex life or attention from other men. This is in no way saying that we cannot be sexual and attractive at any size (we absolutely can). This is around recognising that, for some women, if they feel sexually attractive at whatever magical weight they are aiming for, then achieving their goal may bring up other issues for them. Specifically, they many find themselves significantly overeating when they have already lost a noticeable amount of weight and undoing all of the good work they have done.

Very often the underlying reasons for self-sabotage are not apparent to the person experiencing it (only the feelings of frustration are!). If you feel this may be happening to you, ask yourself:

- If you achieved your goal, what would you then have to do that you currently do not?

- Are there any new challenges or fears you would have to face in light of achieving your goal?

- If you achieved your goal, what excuses would no longer be available to you that you currently use?

Again, the important thing here is self-awareness; if we understand what is happening we are empowered to face our fears and remove the barriers blocking us from our goals.

4 Not valuing our time (and ourselves) enough to say 'no'

As we have discussed throughout this book, many of us, as women, put other's needs before our own and, in doing so, forget to consider what *we* need. One of the most precious, and often undervalued, things we have in life, is time.

The time we have is finite; whilst there are, of course, certain things we understandably feel duty bound to do, if we *constantly* feel our time has been hijacked we need to seriously reconsider how we are spending our time and with whom. Take time to review your diary for the coming month and consider how many things you want to do, how many you need to do and how many you wish weren't doing.

If we do not value our time enough to say 'no' to others, there is a very real danger that we will *never* have enough time to look after ourselves or pursue our own dreams.

5 Fear of standing on our own two feet

As women, many of have us have had phases of our lives when we have had to rely on our partner (emotionally, physically or financially) due to pregnancy and childbirth, bringing up children, our partner's work commitments, illness or life events. It is no wonder then that, when we are planning to make changes, standing on our own two feet can, for some of us, seem daunting.

Whether we are thinking of starting a new course, a new job or, indeed, a whole new life, we need to key into our inner knowledge of who we are; not just who we are as a mother, a wife or a daughter but who we are as an individual. We, each of us, have much more strength, more resilience and more capacity to survive that we are ever aware of. We also have a wonderful ability to experience great joy and fulfilment when we take control of our own destiny.

It is your life; make it everything you truly want it to be

Throughout this book, we have explored the specifics of your life; what is working and what isn't, what makes you happy and what causes you pain, what flows smoothly and what causes you frustration.

Recognising our part in creating the life we are currently living is hugely empowering:

• We *can* choose to make our intimate relationships the best they can be

- We *can* choose to look after ourselves and ensure we are in the best possible physical shape

- We *can* choose to change the roles we take on within our families

- We *can* choose to develop ourselves in ways that are fulfilling and meaningful to us

- We *can* choose to have a home that feels like our own personal sanctuary

- We *can* choose to be surrounded by friends who inspire us and nurture our soul

I wish you every success and happiness in *all* areas of your life; I hope this book has enabled you to review your way of seeing the world and empowered you to change your dance wherever and with whomever you need to. I also hope it has empowered you to step forward and take any action you need to in order to move towards the life you dream of.

May the rest of your journey bring you love, laughter and happiness.

Hester